Three Questions

from your Uncle

Published in the United States by
Maillot Press
P.O. Box 431
Emmitsburg, MD 21727

ISBN 978 0 578 21767 3

Cover design by Laura A. Hullett

To

Audrey

For

Tyrrell, Aline, Nicholas, Christopher, Henry,
Laurel, Charlotte, Grégoire, Ted, Beatrice, Katie,
Helen, Marie, Lawrence, Joseph Andrew, Ian,
Mary Margaret, Sophie, and Monique

Contents

THREE QUESTIONS FROM YOUR UNCLE

"Because the blind cannot see it,
it does not follow that
the sun does not shine."

St. Theophilus of Antioch*

* 2nd century Patriarch of Antioch, born a pagan

1 Preface

Most people are rather easy going about religious and moral matters, some even flippant or dismissive. Granted, scrupulously devout individuals do exist, but such are not the majority of men. Why indeed make such a fuss about whether someone wishes to be an Episcopalian instead of a Catholic, or a Buddhist for that matter or simply a Spiritual (rather than a Religious) Person? And if I am a Catholic, should it not be simply a matter of personal predilection how often I go to Mass or whether I eat fish on Fridays in Lent? And with regard to moral matters, it might be agreed that you could take an interest in my not murdering my boss or robbing a bank, but who are you really to tell me not to use contraception or do myself in once the doctors have thrown up their hands?

When one of those persons suspected of being a religious fanatic is asked on what grounds he concerns himself with the religious beliefs and personal choices of other people, the answer takes some form as this: "because I want you to be happy". To which, the person who is a Buddhist or a playboy or a C & E churchgoer[1] will reply: "but I *am* happy just as I am, thank you". At which point, our zealot needs to be more precise: "I am mainly concerned, you see, about your *eternal* happiness."

Ah, now, the parties to the dialogue, upon reaching this point, have found common ground. Everyone can agree that if there is such a thing as eternal happiness (and eternal unhappiness), this matters more than anything else – more than everything from sleeping in on Sundays to avoiding awkward conversations about other people's business. It is clear enough that for eternal happiness any temporal trouble would be worth enduring. What is not clear, however, and what is, therefore, the subject of this small book is the following:

- Does personal existence really continue after death? (That is, are we immortal?)

- If so, is eternal happiness a possible form that this existence can take?

- If so, what is necessary to ensure that my afterlife will, in fact, take this form?

---

[1] only on Christmas and Easter

Many readers, who have read this far in what is clearly a religious book, have already done something quite unusual. Glancing at how many pages remain and how many unaccustomed arguments will need to be faced may incline them – and you – towards putting the book aside. However, before you do so, please consider those three questions again. No rational human being can fail to ask them. No rational human being can rest easy until they are satisfactorily answered. What are the grounds for your answers? Remember: the subject itself – eternal happiness – is, we can all agree, worth some trouble. Trouble yourself, then, to test your position against that which follows.

CHAPTER I

Is there really personal existence after death? (Or, are we immortal?)

2 A Philosophical Question

2.1 The Atmosphere of Secularism

Human beings have always recognized that life continues after death in some form, as the burial customs of many ancient peoples testify. The body corrupts, beyond all doubt. Therefore, the customs carried out for the benefit of the dead indicate that human beings have generally believed, implicitly, in some kind of soul. With this, no one will argue, but the general attitude of modern secular society is to consider this attitude "pre-scientific". Even if belief in an afterlife remains widespread today, this would simply show the tenacity of cultural legacies, the incoherence or ignorance of the multitude, the power of suggestion, sentiment or wishful thinking. A modern, rational person must admit – the dominant culture tells us – that spiritual beings just do not exist.

Today, many people still speak of God and the soul with a certain respect, but without meaning by these terms anything clearly defined: "God" can just stand for any greater idea or power which affords a person meaning or security, and "soul" can indicate nothing more than a mix of personality, intuition and noble sentiment (e.g. "George had a good soul and a big heart"). Gone is the common conviction that these are genuine realities, with objective meanings: God as a unique, personal, eternal Being and man as a spiritual being who perdures beyond the death of his body. Gone is the presumption that every rational person acknowledges these realities and takes them into account in the ordering of his life and that of society. The atmosphere of secularism has made belief in the spiritual world completely optional, sentimental and therefore private.

Consequently, it is not surprising that many young people either acknowledge these realities with hesitation or deny them altogether. Both the mass media and the majority of schools either ignore the spiritual question entirely, considering it one of private sentiment, or instill prejudices against it. Such is the state we are in, but how did we get here?

2.2   Secularism and Science

Secularism is not a necessary consequence of the development of natural science, but it has accompanied it. Occasionally, one hears claims to the effect that space exploration has not discovered God "out there", nor has molecular biology found any soul lurking in the human body. This sort of comment exemplifies the widespread notion that scientific progress has done away with the need for what are now presumed to be quaint explanations for the existence and attributes of the universe and of man.

A good example of this perspective is provided by the philosopher, John Searle:

> Given what we know about the details of the world – about such things as the position of elements in the periodic table, the number of chromosomes in the cells of different species, and the nature of the chemical bond – this [naturalistic] world view is not an option. It is not simply up for grabs along with a lot of competing world views. Our problem is not that somehow we have failed to come up with a convincing proof of the existence of God or that the hypothesis of an afterlife remains in serious doubt, it is rather that in our deepest reflections we cannot take such opinions seriously. When we encounter people who claim to believe such things, we may envy them the comfort and security they claim to derive from these beliefs, but at bottom we remain convinced that either they have not heard the news or they are in the grip of faith. We remain convinced that somehow they must separate their minds

into separate compartments to believe such things.[2]

So, it is impossible, according to Searle, for persons living in the age of advanced science to "take seriously" the notions of God's existence and of personal immortality. But why? Just because we have identified the elements of the periodic table? Where is the logic in that? Notice, there is a presumption that scientific and religious categories are incompatible, but no argument for it. In fact, the roots of the perception that such an incompatibility exists are so deep that most people, even an intellectual like Searle, are not likely to know where to find them.

Before examining those roots, I note that it is particularly interesting for me that Searle chooses to mention our knowledge of the periodic table of elements as a reason to deny God's existence. In my first year of seminary, a fellow seminarian, who had been a chemistry major at Harvard, gave a short talk on this very theme. His

---

[2] John R. Searle, *The Rediscovery of the Mind* (Cambridge, Mass., and London: MIT Press, 1992), pp. 90-91; cited in Brad S. Gregory, *The Unintended Reformation: How a Religious Revolution Secularized Society* (Cambridge, Mass., and London: Harvard University Press, 2012), p. 27.

goal, which was most memorably achieved, was to show that a consideration of the elements of the periodic table should lead to recognition of the Creator and to admiration of his wisdom and power!

2.3 "Room" for God

What is going on here? Who is blind: the materialist who cannot recognize the hand of God, or the theist who cannot see the self-sufficiency of material reality?

Speaking at the University of Chicago in 1959 for the Centennial celebrations of the publication of Darwin's *The Origin of Species*, Sir Julian Huxley affirmed:

> In the Evolutionary pattern of thought there is no longer either need or room for the supernatural. The earth was not created, it evolved. So did all animals and plants that inhabit it, including our human selves, mind and soul as well as brain and body. So did religion. Evolutionary man can no longer take refuge from his loneliness in the arms of a divinized father figure.[3]

---

[3] Cited in many places including Cardinal Christoph Schönborn's first catechetical lecture for 2005/2006: Sunday, Oct. 2, 2005, St. Stephan's Cathedral, Vienna; see

Let us show, on the contrary, that there is "room" for God and then that there is "need" for him.

In his famous autobiography, the former atheist and Communist spy, Whittaker Chambers, describes the moment of his first inkling that God does in fact exist: contemplating his baby daughter's ear.[4] It struck him as so marvelous and beautiful that it had to have been designed by a great intelligent power. Now, suppose someone, operating with the worldview of Professor Searle or Huxley, were to say "Poppycock! The ear is shaped just that way to maximize the perception of sound, which is useful for survival. We can show you various examples of more primitive ears from which this baby's ear descended by

---

https://zenit.org/articles/cardinal-schonborn-on-creation-and-evolution/, accessed 12 October 2017.

[4] Whittaker Chambers, *Witness*, (Regnery Publishing: Washington, 1987), p. 16. "My eye came to rest on the delicate convolutions of her ear – those intricate, perfect ears. The thought passed through my mind: 'No, those ears were not created by any chance coming together of atoms in nature (the Communist view). They could have been created only by immense design.' The thought was involuntary and unwanted. I crowded it out of my mind. But I never wholly forgot it or the occasion. I had to crowd it out of my mind. If I had completed it, I should have had to say: Design presupposes God. I did not then know that, at the moment, the finger of God was first laid upon my forehead."

chance and natural selection." Now, granting for the moment that such a process of development could be demonstrated, in what way does this conflict with Chambers's intuition? To say that God created the human ear, does not mean that he produced it immediately out of nothing, without any mediation. There is no reason why an omnipotent Creator should not bring forth the ear by means of secondary causes including accidental ones.

Likewise, when a believer praises God for "wine which cheers man's heart" (Ps. 104:15), there is no reason to scoff, while observing that wine is a product of human ingenuity. Certainly it is, but cannot man's role be a cause ordained by God, who, intending to provide this gift – among other reasons, so that His Son could eventually institute the Holy Mass – made grapes with the potential to be turned into wine and made persons clever enough to develop the method? An omnipotent God can work not only through chance causes but free ones, as well.

So, there is "room" for God, provided that one have a sufficiently grand idea of God, that is, of a truly omnipotent, transcendent God. In other words, when John Searle and modern culture reject a notion of "God", they are not rejecting the God of Christian revelation. Unwittingly, they have set up a "straw God"[5] that is easy to knock down. Their "God" would operate like any natural cause. Many simple believers have a true notion of God gleaned from Sacred Scripture: a God who is eternal, living in unapproachable light,[6] and far beyond anything we could understand or imagine. However, when attempts are made to speak of God in precise terms, it is easy for errors to intrude. In fact, it was one of the greatest achievements of St. Thomas Aquinas (1224-1275) to develop a metaphysics which allows one to grasp this point about God more clearly. He taught what is known as "the analogy of being", which expresses the truth that, if all existing things receive their being from God, he must possess being in a different sense. We *participate* in being, but God simply *is*.

We might also recall that the medieval Schoolmen championed the compatibility of philosophy and theology, for all truth is one. In this light, it is marvelous that when Moses asked God his name before the burning bush, God

---

[5] The "straw man" fallacy occurs when one does not actually address one's opponent's argument but a phony version of it.

[6] I Tim. 6:16.

revealed himself as "I am who am".[7] This corresponds perfectly with St Thomas's definition of God as *ipse esse subsistens* (subsistent being itself).

Soon after St. Thomas and the High Middle Ages, at the beginning of the 14th century, a grave philosophical error began to creep into Western thought and with it the germs of the idea that science and religion are somehow incompatible.

As indicated above, the correct notion of God, as the source of all created being, requires that he exist on a completely different level of being than we do. He is self-subsisting, necessary and therefore eternal; we, on the contrary, like all of creation, are brought forth from nothing and could very well not exist at all.[8] Gradually, however, the idea developed that God is part of the same universe as we. This has been called "metaphysical univocalism", in contrast to the "analogy of being" mentioned above. The first step towards modern day atheism was taken unwittingly by Blessed Duns Scotus (1266-1308), who assert-

---

[7] cf. Ex 3:14. The abbreviation for this is YHWH, the most holy Name of God, not to be pronounced by observant Jews.

[8] In philosophical terminology, God is "necessary", and creatures are "contingent".

ed that being must be posited univocally (that is, in the same sense) of God and creation. In this way, God began to be considered as a potential competitor with natural causes, rather than as a transcendent cause, which works through secondary causes without depriving them of their proper nature.

It is vital to keep firmly in mind that God is Being itself, in which all other beings participate.[9] Only on such a view of God are the claims made by believers coherent. For instance, in this light it appears nonsensical to ask whence God originated.[10] Moreover, divine providence is only compat-

---

[9] St. Paul indicated the same to his Athenian audience in the Areopagus: "in him we live and move and have our being" (Acts 17:28).

[10] The following excerpt from Bertrand Russell's famous talk "Why I am not a Christian" shows that both Russell and John Stuart Mill, despite being famous philosophers, had no inkling of the fact that they were operating under the cloud of metaphysical univocalism: "I may say that when I was a young man and was debating these questions very seriously in my mind, I for a long time accepted the argument of the First Cause, until one day, at the age of eighteen, I read John Stuart Mill's Autobiography, and I there found this sentence: 'My father taught me that the question, "Who made me?" cannot be answered, since it immediately suggests the further question, "Who made God?" ' That very simple sentence showed me, as I still think, the fallacy in the argument of the First Cause. If everything must have

ible with chance events and free will if the First cause exists on a diverse level of being.[11] Likewise, miracles are only possible if caused by a transcendent Being, who can ordain events through secondary causes (as when a person heals naturally) or directly (as when a malady is instantly and inexplicably cured). The Deists of the 18th century were adamantly opposed to the possibility of miracles – and so also to the Incarnation of the Son of God – because they operated from a false notion of God as member of the same order of being as nature.

---

a cause, then God must have a cause." On the contrary, God cannot have a cause, if he is Being itself. The assumption that "everything must have a cause" excludes the Christian God – the Eternal God, He Who Is – without argument.

[11] "Nor can the possibility of failure on the part of secondary causes, by means of which the effects of providence are produced, take away the certainty of divine providence, as the *fifth* argument implied. For God Himself operates in all things, and in accord with the decision of His will, as we showed above. Hence, it is appropriate to His providence sometimes to permit defectible causes to fail, and at other times to preserve them from failure." St. Thomas Aquinas, *Summa Contra Gentiles*, III, Chapter 94, n. 16 (trans. Vernon J. Bourke, Notre Dame, IN: Notre Dame Press, 1975.)

2.4 "Need" for God

Even if it be granted that the existence of God is compatible with the entities and forces that are the proper object of the natural sciences, one of the most potent reasons for not believing in God would remain: that he is not necessary. In other words, even if there is "room" for God, we must still show that there is "need" of him.

a. Loss of Metaphysics

Duns Scotus was followed by another thinker who shared his metaphysical univocalism: William of Ockham (1287-1347). Ockham is most famous for his so-called "razor", or the idea that the simplest explanation for a phenomenon should be followed, rather than positing unnecessary entities. This seems both reasonable and unobjectionable, because it is: before Ockham was even born, St. Thomas assumed this notion of parsimony, mentioning it, for instance, as a possible objection to the existence of God.[12] If "Ockham's razor" is not novel, then why is it so famous?

---

[12] "Further, it is superfluous to suppose that what can be accounted for by a few principles has been produced by many." (*ST* I, q. 2, a. 3, obj. 2). St. Thomas Aquinas, in this famous article on the existence of God, only lists two

The answer is clear: it is not the principle that is new but the abandon with which it was applied. Ockham began a trend of viewing metaphysical entities, such as universals,[13] with increasing suspicion, considering them no longer necessary to make sense of the world around us.[14] In fact, a mortal wound was being dealt to

---

arguments against his existence: the reality of evil and the claim that everything can be adequately explained without God.

[13] William of Ockham is best known for being a "nominalist", which means that he denied that there are "universals" or essences common to all the members of a class. Aristotle explained the one-many problem by teaching that all cats, for instance, participate in the same essence, or feline nature, which only exists as instantiated in individual cats. This position, held also by Thomas Aquinas, is called "moderate realism", in contrast to the extreme view of Plato, according to which these essences have a real existence of their own in a different realm.

[14] In reality, Ockham introduced a radically new epistemology, which, in the words of Cambridge historian, David Knowles, "changed the whole landscape of contemporary thought by denying to the philosopher all right to any knowledge of the extra-mental universe save the intuitive knowledge of individual things, each of which was so irreducibly individual as to be unsusceptible of any intelligible relationship or connection with any other individual." The result of this was the destruction of classical metaphysics. "With the dictum *entia non sunt multiplicanda praeter necessitatem* — the so-called 'razor of Ockham' — the most venerable philosophical entities

28

metaphysics, that is, to that part of philosophy, the noblest and highest part, which applies reason to investigating the being and nature of things. For instance, how do things change and yet remain the same? What is it about things that allows us to know anything about them? From pondering such questions, thinkers ever since the Greeks gradually developed the understanding of soul and of God that we now have. For Ockham, however, it seemed doubtful that these realities could be known by reason alone.

b. Development of Science

As Scholastic philosophy waned, Europe passed through other changes, such as the devastating event of the black plague and the schisms in the Church following the Avignon papacy. A cultural

---

could be shorn away. Once Ockham's epistemology had been admitted, realism was doomed, causality was reduced to the observation of happenings and the central concepts of nature and substance disappeared" (cfr. *The Evolution of Medieval Thought*, New York: Vintage Books, 1962, 327-328). This made certain rational knowledge of God and the soul (the "*preambula fidei*") unattainable. The resulting split between reason and faith distorted them both: reason into narrow empiricism and faith into blind fideism (cf. Encyclical Letter of John Paul II, *Fides et Ratio [On the Relationship of Faith and Reason]*, Vatican, 14 September 1998).

renewal began which is known as the Renaissance. Gradually, progress in mathematics and experimental science began to open up a realm of intellectual endeavor that was objectively demonstrable and verifiable. Could not this new method of investigation give mankind all of the knowledge that was worth having?

The natural sciences were attractive not only for the technical benefits they brought, but also for being a realm of thought which was free of controversy. By the mid-sixteenth century, Europe was divided along confessional lines. Protestants tended to reject not only Catholic theology but Scholastic metaphysics, as well. They thought that the effort to use reason to speculate on great questions was impious and unnecessary, if answers could be had from scripture alone. Meanwhile, experimental science was being carried on outside of the universities, clear of controversies about philosophy and religion.

The leading scientific thinkers pursued Descartes's ideal of "clear and distinct ideas", which would be objectively demonstrable and immune to denominational rivalries. Descartes, of course, a philosopher as well as a researcher, and the desire to make philosophy "clear and distinct", like math and experimental science, required the continued application of Ockham's razor. There emerged a great shift in philosophy which gradually seeped into the culture at large. No longer was reality considered far greater than the human mind, which could only gradually discover truth through experience, through speculation (including metaphysics) and through reason enlightened by faith (revealed truth). Henceforth, the human mind was to be the measure of the true and the real: only that which could be clearly and distinctly grasped, verified and demonstrated would be admitted as a proper object of knowledge.[15] Questions of philosophy and morality, no matter how important to the functioning of society would be relegated to the realm of opinion.[16]

----

[15] The logical positivists of the Vienna Circle came to deny intelligibility to any question which could not be answered with empirical methods.

[16] The following example of the anti-metaphysical spirit of our present day has become notorious. In defense of a putative right to abortion, Justice Anthony Kennedy averred: "At the heart of liberty is the right to define one's own concept of existence, of meaning, of the universe, and of the mystery of human life" (cfr. *Planned Parenthood of Southeastern Pennsylvania vs. Casey*, 1992). Alleging the liberty to define one's own concept of such things amounts to a declaration of relativism: that there is no objective truth about the universe and human life.

Ockham's philosophical position has been termed the *via moderna*, and even today he is considered the herald of modernity, since the dismantling of metaphysics has been perceived as a necessary step for the emergence of modern science. However, this view is not accurate. Rather, this is an ideological position that has caused the roots of modern science in the Middle Ages to be overlooked.[17] The limiting of the scope of reason to empirical matters did indeed coincide with dramatic progress in the experimental sciences and in technological advances, but this does not mean that human reason was somehow released from the bonds of metaphysical obscurantism, as is often assumed. Rather, the excitement caused by the advances of empirical science and its utility, together with its immunity from controversy, led to the abandonment of the philosophical interests of earlier centuries. A general limiting of the mind's horizons accompanied the rise of experimental science, and such remains the situation today.

---

[17] Science, as we know it, had its origin in the Middle Ages and, more interestingly, in the Christian theological vision of that period. This thesis has been most effectively advanced through the lifework of Stanley L. Jaki, OSB.

c. Causation and Explanation

In the practical realm of empirical experimentation, it appeared that nature could be viewed as a sort of machine, even if materialism was not explicitly embraced. With regard to Aristotelian metaphysics, this means that two of his four causes came to be ignored or outright denied.[18] Material and efficient causes remained (material objects acting on one another), but formal and final causes fell to the "razor".[19] Formal cause signifies the presence of an essence or nature which is an organizing principle of any entity that is an integrated functioning whole – most obviously, an organism. Final cause indicates purpose: for Aristotle, every agent acts for an end. The nature of a being indicates the sort of action that is proper to it. Admittedly, these are philosophical concepts which are not necessary for making

----

[18] Aristotle introduced the idea, which has remained part of the perennial philosophical tradition, that the understanding of a substance requires four causes: material, formal, efficient and final. One can think of it as the four ways of answering the question "why?" Thus, why is the log burning? Be*cause* it is wood, be*cause* it is porous, be*cause* I lit it, be*cause* it was cold in here.

[19] While most thinkers thought that material and efficient causes were indispensable, David Hume (1711-1776) would question the notion of causation altogether.

scientific discoveries. However, they are necessary to give adequate explanations, rather than mere descriptions and predictions, of the world around us. In other words, while it is fine to dispense with entities that have been multiplied unnecessarily, these Aristotelean insights are not unnecessary.

This point – that the modern mind has grown accustomed to incomplete explanations – is key to recognizing that there really is "need" of God in order to give an adequate explanation of the world.

Design and purpose appear omnipresent in nature (formal and final causes, respectively). Organisms appear to be perfectly made for attaining their goals, be it evading predators or propagating their species. Parts of them also seem marvelously designed for specific purposes, such as ears for hearing. It is quite impossible to speak about nature without speaking "as if" these causes existed, but they are methodologically ruled out in advance. Science can only speak of empirically verifiable realities. This would not be altogether problematic if philosophy were allowed to place the findings of science within the larger context of a rationality open to metaphysics, but, as we have seen, the culture has tended instead to exclude from the realm of objective knowledge anything but the findings of science.[20]

d. Design

It is important to note that design today has a bad reputation, due entirely to the false idea of God

---

[20] Anthony Flew, a philosopher who spent most of his life as an atheist, gives this important insight into why it is so hard for unbelievers to overcome their unbelief: "Now it often seems to people who are not atheists as if there is no conceivable piece of evidence that would be admitted by apparently scientific-minded dogmatic atheists to be a sufficient reason for conceding 'There might be a God after all'. I therefore put to my former fellow-atheists the simple central question: 'what would have to occur or to have occurred to constitute for you a reason to at least consider the existence of a Superior Mind?'" (cf. A. Flew, *There is a God: How the World's most notorious atheist changed his mind*, NY: Harper Collins, 2007, p. 88.)

He says that such persons are like natives who discover a cell phone which produces voices when buttons are pressed. If they rule out in advance that other peoples exist, they try to explain the voices by the combination of buttons, the structure of the instrument, etc. They would say to themselves that it is a more "economical" explanation of the phenomenon to say that the sound is produced by the phone than by "positing" other beings who are speaking. In other words, God is presumed to be impossible before the debate begins. Any non-scientific, in the sense of non-empirically verifiable, knowledge is *ex hypothesi* unacceptable, considered subjective, relative, emotive, and not rational.

explained above (section 2.3). The most famous example of an argument for the existence of God from design is that of William Paley, the 18th century British theologian, who imagined coming across a watch in a field. Upon discovering it, Paley argued, one recognizes immediately that, unlike a stone one might have encountered, the watch must have been made by a watchmaker for the purpose of telling time. This "Divine Watchmaker" argument – that there are elements of nature so complex that we must posit a designer – is essentially proposed today also by supporters of Intelligent Design (ID). In this regard, it is crucial to see that Paley and ID theorists are arguing under the same metaphysical prejudices as their materialist opponents: they are assuming metaphysical univocalism, a God on our level of being. Consequently, such interventions by God to design certain aspects of creatures would be essentially miraculous, outside the course of nature. Classic Aristotelian-Thomistic metaphysics, on the other hand, recognizes that in natural entities, formal and final causes are internal.[21] In

---

[21] "For St. Thomas (again, following Aristotle), the formal and final causes of artifacts, like desks, computers, and iPods are imposed from outside the collection of parts by an intelligent agent. On the other hand, the formal and final

other words, as we saw earlier, a genuinely transcendent God both designs and moves his creation towards its end through the natures that he has created. There is need for an intelligent being to design and direct natural entities, but no need for his intervention in the material universe (although genuine miracles, like the curing of a leper, are still possible). Consequently, the ears of rabbits can develop for the purpose of hearing in a natural manner which biology can study, while being, at the same time, designed by God himself, which philosophy and theology can study. In order to fully explain a natural phenomenon, it is necessary to identify all the causes which produce it, not only those within the scope of experimental science.

In this section, we have attempted to show, contrary to the secularist spirit of the age, that God can and must exist. This was a necessary step towards showing that human beings have souls.

---

causes of natural objects are intrinsic to those objects." Beckwith, Francis J. "Intelligent Design, Thomas Aquinas, and the Ubiquity of Final Causes", The BioLogos Foundation, www.BioLogos.org/projects/schola-essays. Cf. Aristotle, Physics (trans. R. P. Hardie and R. K. Gaye), bk. II, available at http://classics.mit.edu/Aristotle/ physics.2.ii.html. 10. Ibid].

Only if a spiritual, personal God exists, might other spiritual beings also exist, both those without bodies (angels) and those with bodies (human beings).

3 The Human Soul

Personal immortality requires that the human person have a spiritual existence that persists after the death of the body. The understanding of the human person as consisting of body and soul is ancient, although it only gained precision under philosophers familiar with Christian revelation: as just mentioned, the concept of a creator God, who is pure spirit, is a great help to recognizing our own spiritual nature. In modern times, however, it has become decidedly unfashionable to assert that this spiritual reality exists at all.[22]

3.1 Knowledge of the soul by reason and revelation.

The earliest Greek philosophers identified the principle which gives life to living things as the soul. From the Greek word for soul (ψυχή,

---

[22] Nietzsche even speaks of "the great lie of personal immortality" (Der Antichrist, n. 43).

psychē) we get "psychology", and the Latin word for soul (*anima*) is at the root of "animal" and "inanimate". The concept of the soul is a step towards understanding and describing the mystery of life. Indeed, one must stop and wonder at the marvelous capacity that plants and animals have to take in nutrition, grow, move themselves and even reproduce. Just consider a simple bird: a small sparrow. This creature which can fly and chirp and build nests emerged from an egg, which developed inside another bird just like it... Wonder is, as Aristotle remarked, at the origin of philosophy. Part of the inability of the modern mind to appreciate the reality of the soul is surely this loss of wonder; living creatures are assumed to be purely material products of chance. From this dull modern perspective, it only remains to wait until science fully understands the workings of these purposeless machines. Our only interest consists in trying to turn such knowledge to practical, technological advantage.

In truth, however, life is a mystery, and claims that it began spontaneously by chance have not proven convincing.[23] More especially, for the purposes of this book, it must be noted that there are levels of living beings from coral, bacteria and moss up through dogs and humans. There are notable differences among these beings in their capacity to interact with the environment and with regard to self-movement and perception. In particular, in the case of man, there is a chasm between our species and all others, a difference not only of degree but of kind.

Christian philosophers embraced Aristotle's conception that the soul is the "form" of the body, that is, its organizing principle. This philosophical understanding has been confirmed by the Magisterium[24] as illuminating what revelation tells us about the human person.[25] While Aristotle did not clearly assert the spiritual nature of the soul, further philosophical reflection has clarified the issue, as we will see.

---

[23] cf. Jonathan Wells, *Icons of Evolution: Science or Myth*, (Washington, DC: Regnery Publishing, 2000), Chapter 2 "The Miller-Urey Experiment", p. 9-28.

[24] This term refers to the leaders of the Catholic Church when exercising their teaching role.

[25] cf. Council of Vienne in 1312 (DS 902) and CCC 365.

3.2 Characteristics of the Soul

The soul distinguishes us from all the other living creatures[26] by making us intelligent, a "rational animal" or *homo sapiens*. The soul also accounts for our ability to make free choices. It enables us to love, entering into relationships with other spiritual beings, including God. Today, there is a great deal of effort spent by biologists to emphasize what humans and animals have in common.[27] Attempts are made to teach animals grammar, to show that certain species use tools, play games, care for the dead, and so on. Certainly, studying such behaviors can lead to a greater knowledge of animal life, but it cannot show that the difference between humans and animals is one only of degree.[28] Again, the inability to wonder shows

---

[26] cf. Gen. 2:18-20.

[27] Blaise Pascal: "He is neither angel, nor beast, but man... It is dangerous to show man too much how he is like beasts, without showing him his grandeur. It is also dangerous to show him too much his grandeur without his lowliness. It is still more dangerous to let him ignore one or the other. But it is very advantageous to put in evidence both the one and the other" (*Pensées*, édit. Brunschvicg, n. 140).

[28] Medieval thinkers already noted the marvelous "sagacity" of animals, such as the fact that hunting dogs, coming to a three-way fork in pursuit of a deer, will sniff the first and second paths and will then, if the scent has not yet

itself: this time to wonder at "What a piece of work is a man!"[29] One can see, of course, that both man and birds build homes for themselves. One can also marvel at the ingenuity of birds' nests. But is it not blindingly obvious that man creates an infinite variety of architectural styles by reason and will, while birds of a given species make the nests they do inevitably, by innate instinct?

Indeed, if modern culture were not experiencing a crisis in philosophical thinking, people would immediately see the contradiction in the very notion of "material beings thinking". The desire to explain natural phenomena in the simplest manner possible became a tendency to eliminate all causes that could not be experimentally verified. Here Ockham's razor returns, cutting out metaphysical principles which are genuinely necessary to explain our experience. The human mind was gradually assumed to be

---

been discovered, take off on the third path without sniffing it (cf. St. Thomas Aquinas, ST I-II, q. 13, art. 2, obj. 3).

[29] "How noble in reason! how infinite in faculty! in form, in moving, how express and admirable! in action how like an angel! in apprehension how like a god! the beauty of the world! the paragon of animals! And yet, to me, what is this quintessence of dust?" (from William Shakespeare, *Hamlet*, Act II, Scene ii).

nothing but chemicals and electricity, essentially a computer. Advances in information technology and artificial intelligence have only increased the category confusion between "automated reasoning" and natural intelligence. Nonetheless, everyone intuitively acknowledges that typically human actions – such as falling in love – are much more than mere chemical interactions.[30] That persons can convince themselves otherwise shows how far modern man has gone in losing a sense of the mystery, wonder and beauty of existence.

We have noted that there are many operations that only the human being is capable of. As Fr Aleksander Men said, "no living creature apart from man has ever pondered the meaning of life, risen above natural physical necessity, or demonstrated the capacity to risk his life for the sake of Truth or that which he cannot grasp in his

---

[30] While Stephen Pinkers argues that the human being is an element of a purposeless world, as much a product of chance and evolutionary processes as any plant or animal, he inexplicably announces at one point: "*People* have goals, of course, but projecting goals onto the workings of nature is an illusion" (cf. *Enlightenment Now: the Case for Reason, Science, Humanism, and Progress*, [New York: Random House, 2018], p. 24). Is there something greater than matter in man or not?

hand."[31] This thought prepares the way to grasp the philosophical proofs that this capacity of man requires a non-material component. Naturally, such proofs will not be easily grasped in a culture in which the study of metaphysics has been ignored and ridiculed for many centuries. In fact, one of the key arguments for the spirituality of the soul builds upon the very concept of universals which Ockham wished to eliminate with his "razor". Understanding is essentially grasping the essence of things – recognizing this object as a triangle, for instance, by grasping the defining properties of a triangle, in such a way that any triangle could be identified as such. While material sense perception can perceive the characteristics of the concrete individual, only a spiritual faculty could perceive the abstract concept, common to a species or class. This notion is at the origin of the word "intelligent", which implies an ability to "read within" (*intus-legere*), perceiving the universal essence beneath the characteristics of this particular member of a class.

---

[31] from the last lecture, 8 Sept. 1990, of an Orthodox priest in Saint Petersburg, before being assassinated the next day, presumably by atheistic communist agents.

In this life, we need the brain to think, but it is no more than an instrumental cause of our understanding, which is accomplished primarily by the rational soul. (Analogously, one may not be able to see without glasses, but the power of sight is in the eyes). The fact that persons are a body/soul unity means that it is to be expected that spiritual acts (say, playing chess) should have corresponding material effects (measurable activity in a certain part of the brain). However, the ability of neuroscientists to observe and describe these effects is not the same as explaining the phenomenon. Likewise, damage to the brain, will prevent the spiritual soul from exercising its operations through the body. Nonetheless, a person in a persistent vegetative state, or an embryo before the brain is even formed, has a soul and thus the very same human dignity as a person with a working brain.[32] This same fact — that the soul is fully present and operative in a person whose body is only a "clump of cells" — helps us see that the soul can be fully present and

---

[32] One should recall, in this connection, the testimony of persons who subsequently recount hearing and understanding perfectly the conversations of those around them during a time when they had been declared "brain dead" (for example, see "Surprising Realities of Brain Death and Organ Donation", Part I, in *Facing Life Head On* Series).

operative after death, as well. Thanks to the immaterial soul, we have a personal existence which continues after the dissolution of our body. We are naturally immortal.

As a purely spiritual reality, the soul cannot be generated biologically, but must be created immediately by God.[33] While the Church has not declared that conception is the moment when the soul is united to the body, this has become philosophically ever more clear, as knowledge of the biology of procreation has progressed.[34] The

---

[33] cf. Pius XII, *Humani Generis* (DS 3896) and CCC 366. For this reason, God must create new souls individually each time a new human life comes into existence. The parents' cooperation with God in this process is called "procreation". Eve, the first woman ever to conceive, expressed this truth by exclaiming: "I have begotten a child with the help of the Lord" (Gen. 4:1).

[34] cf. Congregation for the Doctrine of the Faith, *Donum Vitae*, I, 1 (22 February 1987): "Certainly no experimental datum can be in itself sufficient to bring us to the recognition of a spiritual soul; nevertheless, the conclusions of science regarding the human embryo provide a valuable indication for discerning by the use of reason a personal presence at the moment of this first appearance of a human life: how could a human individual not be a human person? The Magisterium has not expressly committed itself to an affirmation of a philosophical nature, but it constantly reaffirms the moral condemnation of any kind of procured abortion. This teaching has not been changed and is unchangeable."

soul is the principle needed to guide the process of development. The fact that the human soul is spiritual, that is, immaterial, and infused by God, makes us to be created "in the image and likeness of God".[35] This is the source of the inviolable dignity of every human person no matter how small, weak, handicapped or sick. It is the ground of what we call today the "sanctity of life". For our purposes, it is also the ground of the personal immortality and transcendent destiny of each and every human being.

---

[35] cf. Gen. 1:26.

CHAPTER II

Is eternal happiness a possible form
that this existence can take?

4   Christian view of the afterlife

4.1   Revelation needed

Our discussion thus far, concerning the existence of an immortal soul, has been philosophical. Now, as we consider the nature of life after death and how to prepare for it, we must turn to theology. The former is the domain of reason, the latter of reason operating together with faith.

We described in part one how a narrowing of the scope of reason has occurred over several centuries which has led to the neglect of much of traditional philosophy.[36] This process has led to an even harsher judgment on religious faith. An attitude is now commonplace according to which faith is unreasonable, as expressed for instance by Steven Pinkers in his bestseller, *Enlightenment Now*: "To take something on faith means to believe it without good reason, so by definition a faith in the existence of supernatural entities

---

[36] "Scientism" refers to the idea that the only real knowledge is that which comes from science. Usually, this is an unconscious bias, but sometimes it is explicitly affirmed, as in this remark of Bertrand Russell: "what science cannot discover, mankind cannot know" (B. Russell, *Religion and Science*, New York: Oxford University Press, 1961, p. 243).

clashes with reason."[37] The irony is that such an adamant defense of reason actually fails to appreciate human reason sufficiently. Reason is capable of much more than the analysis of concrete problems which fit properly within the purview of science. It is capable of speculating on great questions having to do with the underlying causes and purposes of all that exists. It is made for wonder, wisdom and contemplation, not simply analysis and deduction. This leads to an interesting and important paradox: *recognizing the true scope and grandeur of human reason also means confronting its limits*. Having understood himself to be part of created nature, man will have to admit that he cannot plumb the depths of the reality from which nature comes. Reason recognizes, therefore, that many truths can only be known if they are revealed to us and that it is reasonable that the Creator would be able and willing to do so.

Philosophical wisdom should be compatible with theological doctrine, since truths, however they come to be known, cannot contradict each other (truth just is the way things really are). Pre-Christian cultures developed traditions about

---

[37] Pinkers, S., *Enlightenment Now*, p. 30.

what might await the soul, but they necessarily fall short of the truth. While some cultures hypothesized a return to this life in another form (reincarnation), others imagined some other world to which the soul had to journey in some fashion. These were only guesses: while we can arrive by reason at the fact of immortality, we need to be informed by Another about the actual nature of our existence after death.

The appeal to divine revelation at this point might strike the reader as disappointing, just as a *deus ex machina* plot twist seems to reveal a poor playwright. Is it not too convenient that the very questions which are beyond reason should be answered by divine intervention? How do we know that the Christian view of the afterlife is not a human generated hypothesis like reincarnation or the land beyond the Styx, only a good deal more sophisticated?

Reason cannot prove that those matters which need to be revealed are true; if it could, their revelation would not be necessary.[38] How-

---

[38] Reason still plays a great role in receiving, grasping and communicating revealed truths. To say that we just "take something on faith" is misleading, for reason is more needed than ever to work through the many problems that arise from revealed data. For instance, Jesus Christ reveals

ever, reason can provide what are called "arguments of convenience (or fittingness)". It is certainly reasonable that a God who created the human race should have done so for the purpose of sharing his life with men. Moreover, it is certain that, if man could not know about this possibility or how to attain it, his creative plan would be frustrated. Thus, it is reasonable that if eternal life were a possibility, God would reveal all the knowledge and provide all the helps necessary for us to enter into that life. It also follows that this sharing in the life of the One from whom all of the wonders and beauties of nature come must be happy indeed.

4.2   Christ reveals our destiny.

The precise nature of our destiny was only revealed by Jesus Christ. It is not sufficiently noticed how new, vividly detailed and shocking was the information given by Our Lord on this

---

himself as fully God and fully man, yet this raises myriad questions in our minds. With the help of the Holy Spirit, believers, and especially theologians, ponder them and make progress in understanding. As Blessed Cardinal John Henry Newman wrote: "Ten thousand difficulties do not make one doubt" (*Apologia pro vita sua*, London: Longman, 1878, p. 239).

question. It has become so familiar that we forget that once it was new.

Specifically, Christ spoke of a judgment which would divide all people into two radically different groups, which would receive either an eternal reward or an everlasting punishment. The former are called "elect" or "saved", while the latter are referred to as "damned" or "reprobate". The reward – entrance into the Kingdom of God, or heaven – is described as unimaginable happiness or "beatitude". The happiness of heaven consists chiefly in the vision of God, our supreme good. The essential pain of hell is the loss of contact with Him, even though this is expressed in images, especially that of fire, indicating a place of torment and misery. These notions were present in Jewish revelation but only vaguely.

Christ also confirmed the resurrection of the dead, that is, the reuniting of our bodies to our souls at the end of the world, which was a debated question among the Jews of his day. The Islamic notion of the afterlife, wherein the happiness of heaven is thought to consist largely in carnal gratification, is a grave distortion of Christian teaching. In fact, while the happiness of the person will be augmented after the resurrection, the glorified body will share in the joy of the soul. It will know a happiness entirely unlike any human experience: "What no eye has seen, nor ear heard, nor the heart of man conceived, God has prepared for those who love him".[39] Therefore, *pace* the Koran, while our senses will share in spiritual delights, there will be none of the physical pleasures characteristic of this life.

4.3   *Confirmations*

Our primary reason for believing in the possibility of eternal happiness for our immortal souls is the promises of Christ. The credibility of the witness of Jesus Christ – he said that he had come "to bear witness to the truth"[40] – rests upon many sources: the fulfillment of Old Testament prophecies, his extraordinary words and marvelous works recorded in the Gospel, his Resurrection which was both predicted and witnessed, and the history changing effects of his brief ministry.

Since the time of Christ, and the end of public revelation, there have been confirmations of the reality of heaven and hell. Regarding heaven, one can point to the experience of mystics. These

---

[39] I Cor. 2:9
[40] Jn. 18:37

are persons, both men and women, who have progressed extremely far in the way of prayer.[41] Although a small group of chosen souls, they undergo such thorough purifications in this life that they enter into a profound union with God, which is the very foretaste of heaven. While they are unable to put their experiences adequately into words, they do attest to having tasted ineffable happiness, already in this life, for which they would be willing to die a thousand deaths.

In addition, certain persons – again a rare few – have received visits from souls in heaven, from the Mother of God herself (most famously, at Guadalupe, Lourdes and Fatima) and even from the Lord Jesus. These events have proven absolutely inexplicable in natural terms. Visions have not only given evidence of the beauty, peace and joy of heaven, but also of the suffering of the

---

[41] For instance, St. Teresa of Avila writes: "But I can't describe what is felt when the Lord gives [the soul] an understanding of His secrets and grandeurs, the delight that so surpasses all those knowable here on earth; indeed, it rightly makes you abhor the delights of this life, which together are all rubbish. I would find it revolting to have to make a comparison between the two delights, even if those of earth were to last forever and those given by the Lord were only a drop of water from the vast overflowing river that is prepared for us" (*Life*, chapter 27.12).

damned, so that these saints, too, can give witness to the world of the opposing destinies that await souls after death.

These two eventualities – heaven and hell – are so different that they are contrasted as life and death. Heavenly beatitude, which is a sharing in the very life of God, is usually described as "eternal life", whereas the existence of the damned is called "the second death".[42] This should not cause confusion regarding the question of natural immortality, shared equally by the elect and the damned.

4.4   A new perspective

Clearly, these considerations will radically affect one's outlook on life. The years that one spends on earth cannot compare to the unending span of our afterlife. The brief period of earthly life, "seventy years or eighty for those that are strong"[43], followed by judgment,[44] takes on the character of a test. It is an opportunity to ready ourselves to live forever with God and to earn the

---

[42] Rev. 20:14
[43] Ps. 90:10
[44] Heb 9:27: "...it is appointed for men to die once, and after that comes judgement..."

crown of life that He wishes to give us.[45] This perspective determines the behavior of a wise man.[46]

Likewise, the trials of this life take on an entirely new aspect: "I consider that the sufferings of this present time are not worth comparing with the glory that is to be revealed to us."[47] Our life becomes a pilgrimage (we are *viatores* or "way-

---

[45] Jas. 1:12. Like St Paul, we should "straining forward to what lies ahead,… press on toward the goal for the prize of the upward call of God in Christ Jesus" (Phil. 3:13, 14).

[46] "If you are wise, then, know that you have been created for the glory of God and your own eternal salvation. This is your goal; this is the center of your life; this is the treasure of your heart. If you reach this goal you will find happiness. If you fail to reach it, you will find misery. May you consider truly good whatever leads you to your goal and truly evil whatever makes you fall away from it. Prosperity and adversity, wealth and poverty, health and sickness, honors and humiliations, life and death, in the mind of the wise man, are not to be sought for their own sake, nor avoided for their own sake. But if they contribute to the glory of God and your eternal happiness, then they are good and should be sought. If they detract from this, they are evil and must be avoided." (St. Robert Bellarmine, Grad. 1: *Opera omnia* 6, edit. 1862, 214).

[47] Rom. 8:18

farers"), and our attention should logically be kept carefully fixed upon our goal.[48]

4.5   The Fall and the hope of restoration

The Bible also reveals to us the story of the Fall of Man in the first chapters of Genesis. In a sense, the journey of every human being is from that fallen state in which we are conceived towards a restoration of original harmony with God in the new Eden or "paradise"[49] of heaven. These two supra-historical realities – original justice and a final judgment – are necessary to make sense of the present, as the novelist Alessandro Manzoni observed:

> The revelation of a past, of which man carries in himself the sad evidence, without having the tradition or the secret, and of a future, of which we have only confused ideas of terror and desire, renders clear the present, which we have beneath our eyes; the mysteries reconcile the contradictions,

---

[48] Col. 3:2 "Set your mind on things that are above, not on things that are on earth."

[49] In Greek, "paradise" means garden and is the word used for the Garden of Eden.

and visible things are understood through knowledge of the invisible ones.[50]

The human condition – with all of its nobility and sanctity, cruelty and inhumanity – makes more sense in this suprahistorical context, than it does if reduced to a story of random chemicals, self-organizing themselves in a meaningless battle against entropy.

5   Salvation is only through Jesus Christ

5.1   Mystery hidden from the ages

If one recognizes that the human race was created for communion with God but experienced a primordial fall from His friendship, it is evident that the restoration of this relationship could only come by the initiative of God Himself. Here, it is

---

[50] Manzoni, Alessandro *Osservazioni sulla morale cattolica*, vedi "Al lettore". Fratelli Rechiedi, Milano, 1881 (from Wikisource 09/11/2016): "La rivelazione d'un passato, di cui l'uomo porta in sè le triste testimonianze, senza averne da sè la tradizione e il segreto, e d'un avvenire, di cui ci restavano solo idee confuse di terrore e di desiderio, è quella che ci rende chiaro il presente che abbiamo sotto gli occhi; i misteri concilano le contradizioni, e le cose visibili si intendono per la notizia delle cose invisibili."

essential to remember the metaphysical chasm that separates creature and Creator (see 2.3 "Room for God"). This is expressed by the terms "natural" and "supernatural". There is no way for nature to rise up to the supernatural level unless it is somehow elevated by God. Put another way, there is no way that a being who is so infinitely inferior to the Almighty could enter into relationship with Him or share in His life, unless this privilege were granted to him.

The necessity for divine intervention in salvation should be abundantly obvious. The manner in which it was achieved, however, is both marvelous and extraordinary.

5.2 The Incarnation

No one could ever have imagined or suspected the manner in which God chose to save us. The way was prepared by the Jewish prophets, but then an angel sent by God to a young virgin of Nazareth announced that the time had come: she would bear a child who would be God's very Son. By uniting human nature to the divine nature in His person, Jesus Christ renewed fallen humanity. In our human nature, He offered to God a life of perfect service, culminating in His death on the Cross, by which, on behalf of every man, He showed a perfectly unselfish, generous and obedient love for His Heavenly Father. By dying, Jesus offered a perfect sacrifice for sins, and by rising from the dead He conquered death – the punishment of sin. He was sinless, of course, so He did this not for Himself but for every man who ever was or will be born, all of whom share in that grave imperfection, which we call "original sin". By truly becoming a man himself, Christ united Himself to every man and redeemed ("bought back") every one of them.

6   Eternal life is possible

Thus, Jesus Christ opened the way to eternal life: "I am the way, and the truth, and the life; no one comes the Father but through me".[51] However, we saw earlier that He spoke of two distinct possible destinies for us after death. He described the separation which takes place as that between sheep and goats, wheat and tares, and so forth. We must ponder this fact more deeply before, in chapter three, considering what is required to reach life securely.

---

[51] Jn. 14:6.

6.1   Sanctifying grace

One might wonder why the human race is to be divided into two groups for all eternity. Why should there not be a gradation of 10, or even 50, possible destinies, from eternal misery to eternal bliss? In fact, there are gradations both in heaven and in hell, levels of beatitude and levels of wretchedness, respectively; this is only reasonable. Yet, there is necessarily an infinite chasm between the two realms for the very important reason alluded to above: God is completely other.

If we recognize the infinite gulf between the creature and the Creator, the only way that it can be bridged is by a gift of God, which we call grace. This is something which, indeed, can be possessed in varying degrees, but one either has it or one does not. If one has it when one dies, one is united to the Supreme Good and will continue to be so for all eternity, but if one does not, one can never regain His friendship.

God can purify and elevate us so that we can have a "certain equality with God" and enjoy friendship with Him. He is all-powerful, after all, and created us for this. "This is the will of God", St

Paul tells us, "your sanctification".[52] We call grace "sanctifying" because it makes us like God, or "holy". St. Peter says that it makes us "partakers in the divine nature".[53] The Fathers of the Church even spoke of it as the "divinization" of man. This is possible because man is created "in the image of God" as St. Augustine explains: "Due to the fact that the soul is made in the image of God, it is capable of God by grace".[54]

6.2 Grace and Free Will

However, even though God is all-powerful, He cannot force us to accept His love or love Him in return. We remain capable of resisting grace. This follows from the nature of love and friendship, which must be truly free. For this reason, Saint Augustine said "God created us without us, but He did not will to save us without us".[55]

Nonetheless, we must admit that salvation remains entirely a gift from God; that is to say, even the ability to accept His grace is His gift. Of

---

[52] I Thess. 4:3.

[53] 2 Pet. 1:4.

[54] "Eo ipso quod facta est [anima] ad imaginem Dei, capax est Dei per gratiam", cited by St. Thomas, ST I-II, q. 5, a. 1.

[55] *Sermo.* 169, 11, 13. PL 38, 923. Cited in CCC 1847.

course, this presents our limited reason with various conundrums which have caused long and protracted debates and not a few heresies in the history of the Church. The solution, which remains shrouded in mystery, lies once again in a genuine conception of God as the source of our contingent being; thus, He is able to move our wills without depriving us of freedom; indeed, His grace, which causes us to accept Him, makes us freer to do so. Contrary to what we might think, the maximum freedom will be found in being unable to choose anything but God, not in being able to reject Him.

"All is grace", in the dying words of St. Thérèse of Lisieux. It is possible to say that the names of the elect are already written in the Book of the Lamb (cf. Rev. 21:27), and yet we must maintain that all those who will eventually be lost could have been saved, and all those who will eventually be saved could have been lost. The former have only themselves to blame, the latter only the merciful God to thank.[56]

---

[56] The technical terms, "efficacious" and "sufficient" grace, have arisen. Everyone is given sufficient grace to be saved, but only those who actually do cooperate are said to have received efficacious grace. The error to avoid (which the Calvinists failed to avoid) is to think that God predes-

6.3 A real drama

It follows that every human person who has ever lived is involved in a real drama in which his eternal happiness is at stake. In some cases, such as babies or handicapped persons, God's gift of grace is obtained by the free choice of others, who baptize them, or, we may well hope, God shows them mercy in some other way. Most of us, however, are invited to engage, consciously and freely, in a lifelong struggle which will either

---

tines some persons to hell. No, those who reject Him defect through the use of their own liberty. It is true that God permits this and that He could have prevented it, but this is not the same as causing or determining them to perish. This does, however, imply that God loves some persons more than others, which is a difficult doctrine for many to accept. Fr. Reginald Garrigou-Lagrange explains: "But of two men, equally tempted, if one does not resist grace and the other does, the first is better. Therefore he is better because God wills greater good to Him. In other words, the principle of predilection (nobody is better than another unless he is better loved by God) presupposes grace to be efficacious of itself and not from our consent." (cf. his book *Grace*, chap. 7). It remains true that God wills all men to be saved (cf. I Tim 2.4) but in a certain sense: God does not will any sin at all, and yet He permits us the freedom to commit them. (cf. ST I, q. 19, a. 6, ad 1: "Whatever God wills absolutely is done, although what He wills antecedently may not be done.")

be crowned with victory or crushed by defeat at the close of our days.

As we have seen, in this drama God's gift of grace is decisive, as is the freedom of each individual. Nonetheless, other people and circumstances have their role to play. Third parties – parents, friends, teachers, for instance, and the general culture – can either encourage, facilitate, and intercede for us, or they can tempt, scandalize and obstruct our progress. Angels, too, both good and bad, can influence us without restricting our freedom. Other factors, as well, which do not depend upon our choice, such as temperament, class, and chance occurrences, may also favor or prejudice our ability to respond to grace. All of these factors are part of God's providence, presenting each human person with a unique challenge of responding to His offer of salvation. It is key to grasp that while life is not fair, no one fails to reach God except through his own free choice.

6.4   Failure is a real possibility

In these pages, we have been concerned to demonstrate that eternal happiness is a possible form that our immortal life could take. I hope that this goal has been achieved. Before concluding this second chapter of our study, it is also necessary to show that success is *only* a possibility, not a sure thing.

This might seem unnecessary since our knowledge of the possible forms of life after death comes from Jesus Christ, and He clearly spoke of those who go to eternal ruin in the indicative mood. Therefore, one would think that Christians consider ending up in hell to be a distinctly real danger, as artistic depictions of the final judgment have sometimes graphically indicated. In fact, however, influential theological voices have recently been raised arguing that very few persons, or perhaps even no one, will turn out to have failed to reach heaven. These thinkers begin from the observation that the Church has never declared that any particular person, such as Judas, is in hell, nor has she *explicitly* interpreted the Lord's words to mean that some souls have or will effectively be damned. But, of course, there never was a need for such an interpretation by the Magisterium, as no one had ever raised the issue until these thinkers did so beginning in the 1950's.[57]

---

[57] There was a similar heresy in the early Church, which suggested that hell would not be eternal. Modern universal-

In fact, this fairly recent turn towards universalism in eschatology[58] would appear to be little more than an accommodation of distinctly modern attitudes. The trends of relativism and pluralism lead people to think that all religions and cultures are equally salvific. The democratic sense of fairness resists denying equal access to eternal life to everyone. Moreover, strong currents from psychology and sociology argue against imputing any unworthy behavior to personal responsibility. Any genuinely good and merciful God would – the thinking goes – find an excuse for just about anyone, especially if, as we observed above, he could have sent them more grace or other helps towards salvation in the first place.

Here, yet again, we see the fatal habit of reducing God to the level of a creature, which now must follow calculations based on contemporary human standards. But, "who has known the mind of God? Who has been his counselor?"[59]

---

ists, in contrast, admit that hell is eternal, but just doubt that anyone actually goes there.

[58] the theology of the Last Things: death, judgement, heaven and hell.

[59] Rom. 11:34.

Is not "the foolishness of God wiser than men"?[60] Our affection for persons who appear to us to be jolly, fine human beings tells us nothing about the degree of genuine charity in their hearts. God alone can judge who is worthy to stand in his presence. He alone knows why he distributes his gifts as he does, and what will best serve the ultimate, glorious outcome of this massive, multi-billion year adventure designed to provide citizens for the "new heavens and the new earth".[61]

So, having shown that there is a possibility for anyone to reach eternal life, but a need for each one to cooperate actively, let us turn to the final question: in what does that cooperation consist?

---

[60] I Cor 1:25.
[61] Rev. 21:1.

CHAPTER III

What is necessary to ensure that my
afterlife will, in fact, take this form?

7   Applying the merits won by Christ

7.1   The Church

If the guiding principle of our first chapter was reason (metaphysical reason, as opposed to a narrow, empirical rationality), and that of the second chapter was faith (as the topic surpassed what unaided human reason can know), our lodestar for this third chapter is the Magisterium of the Catholic Church. It is not only reasonable, but also incontestable as an historical fact, that the human mind's efforts to receive, grasp and communicate the revelation of Christ will result in a variety of understandings. To some extent, the greatness of the mystery bears varying, complementary perspectives and requires a development of doctrine, as it becomes gradually better appropriated. However, errors and heresies will also arise, leading to schisms or divisions in the one body of Christ's disciples. Hence, there is today a quantity of Christian denominations, each claiming with more or less confidence to present the true teaching of Jesus Christ.

Is it not reasonable that the Lord would have anticipated this eventuality and provided for it? Within ten days of his Ascension into Heaven

He sent down the Holy Spirit upon the Apostles He had chosen, having told them that this Spirit would "guide them into all truth".[62] He had had the foresight to designate among the pillars of his Church a leader, Peter, "the Rock upon which I will build my Church".[63] And He affirmed that this Spirit-led hierarchy would have the role of spreading his teaching,[64] with His own authority: "He who listens to you, listens to me".[65] The successors of the Apostles, with and under the successor of Peter, gradually set forth the fundamental elements of revealed truth, sometimes with the help of ecumenical councils, that is, gatherings of bishops from all over the world. Hence, we now have Creeds, Catechisms and other instruments (a key one being the liturgy[66]) which reliably transmit the "deposit of faith" to succeeding generations.

---

[62] Jn. 16:13.

[63] Mt. 16:18.

[64] "Go, therefore, and teach all nations, baptizing them in the name of the Father, and of the Son, and of the Holy Ghost: Teaching them to observe all things whatsoever I have commanded you." (Mt. 28:19-20); see also Mk. 16:15-16.

[65] Lk. 10:16.

[66] according to the famous adage: *lex orandi lex credenda* (the rule of prayer is the rule of faith).

It is [the Church's] duty to serve humanity in different ways, but one way in particular imposes a responsibility of a quite special kind: the *diakonia of the truth*... [which] obliges the believing community to proclaim the certitudes arrived at, albeit with a sense that every truth attained is but a step towards that fullness of truth which will appear with the final Revelation of God: 'For now we see in a mirror dimly, but then face to face. Now I know in part; then I shall understand fully' (1 Cor 13:12).[67]

7.2 What must I do to be saved?

"Brothers, what must we do?" This anguished question came forth from the crowd, which heard St. Peter's first preaching on the morning of Pentecost, ten days after Jesus ascended into Heaven. He responded: "Repent, and be baptized every one of you in the name of Jesus Christ for the forgiveness of your sins; and you shall receive the gift of the Holy Spirit. For the promise is to you and to your children and to all that are far off, every one whom the Lord our God calls to him.... Save yourselves from this crooked generation."[68]

---

[67] *Fides et Ratio*, n. 2. Note "diakonia" means "service".
[68] Acts 2:37-40.

7.3 Repentance

The first step needed to take hold of the offer of eternal life is "to repent", literally, according to the Greek: "to have a new mind".[69] This was also the essence of Christ's first preaching as recorded by St Mark: "Repent and believe the good news".[70] This is the original grace: an awareness that I am going in the wrong direction, that I cannot please God by my own power, and so I need to be saved. One must respond to this grace at once, for there is no guarantee that multiple opportunities will be given: "Do not delay to turn to the Lord nor postpone it from day to day; for suddenly the wrath of the Lord will go forth, and at the time of punishment you will perish".[71]

7.4 Faith and Baptism

Turning towards the Lord with an open and docile mind allows the person to receive the gift of faith. Belief consists in an act of the will moved by grace, by which a person affirms that Jesus Christ is the Son of God and accepts Him as Savior and

---

[69] metanoia.
[70] Mark 1:15.
[71] Sirach 5:7.

Lord.[72] By this act of faith, the saving death of Christ is applied to the believer. We say that he has been "justified" and raised up to friendship with God by sanctifying grace. He has passed from death to life, for, indeed, the eternal life of which we have spoken is the definitive fulfillment of that which begins now in this life through faith: "This is eternal life: that they know thee the only true God, and Jesus Christ whom thou hast sent".[73]

From the very first days, by the will of Christ, the act of faith was publicly ratified by submitting to the ceremony of baptism. In this very concrete way, at the moment that water is poured over the head as an efficacious sign of the cleansing of sins and as the Name of the Trinity is

---

[72] The mind is not bound to accept revealed truth, as it is bound to accept the conclusion of a mathematical proof. It requires an act of the will: "the intellect is moved by the command of the will to assent to what is of faith: *for no man believeth, unless he will*" (St Thomas Aquinas, ST I-II, q. 56, a. 3, citing Augustine, Tract. xxvi. in Joan.). Nonetheless, this is not a "blind leap", but a reasonable step based upon an examination of motives of credibility. In fact, it is conjectured by St Thomas that the devils, who have a superior intellect to ours, "are, in a way, compelled to believe, by the evidence of signs, and so their will deserves no praise for their belief" (ST II-II, q. 5, a. 2, ad 1).

[73] John 17:3.

invoked, the one being baptized is transformed into a new creature, filled with grace, made a child of God and heir to eternal life. As the citation from St Peter's Pentecost homily indicates, the person is also filled with the Holy Spirit.[74]

Because this new life is an unmerited gift, even babies can be baptized, on the understanding that the faith of their parents and godparents will be shared with them. As soon as their mind develops, they can begin living the full Christian life, appropriating for themselves the privilege and responsibility of being a Christian. Through baptism, we enter the Catholic Church, as through a door,[75] for the Church really is nothing other than the coming together[76] of all those who believe in Christ. He is the unique Savior, the Only Son of God,[77] whose mercy is received by faith.[78]

---

[74] Also Romans 5:5: "The love of God is poured into our hearts through the Holy Spirit who is given to us."

[75] cf. *Lumen Gentium*, n. 14, of the Second Vatican Council.

[76] The etymology of the word for "church" in Greek and Latin (= ecclesia) indicates a calling-forth, a coming together of persons into one community.

[77] "there is no other name given to men by which we are to be saved". Acts 4:12.

The Church is, as it were, the antechamber of heaven, for her members already enjoy eternal life in a real, if inchoate and insecure manner. The Second Vatican Council describes her as "the seed and beginning of the Kingdom [of God] on earth".[79] It is not surprising, therefore, that the Church is presented as a sort of ark in the flood, necessary for salvation. The ancient formula – *extra Ecclesiam nulla salus*[80] or "outside the Church there is no salvation" – remains true in our day, as the Second Vatican Council taught: "Whosoever, therefore, knowing that the Catholic Church was made necessary by Christ, would refuse to enter or to remain in it, could not be saved." (*Lumen Gentium*, n. 14). It is important to note, however, that those persons might still be

---

[78] "[Christ] became the source of eternal salvation for all who obey him". Heb. 5:9.

[79] "huiusque Regni in terris germen et initium constitu-it", *Lumen Gentium* 5.

[80] This is a famous expression drawn from St. Cyprian, which is a dogma of the faith. In 1215, the Lateran Council IV included it in a definition of the Catholic faith against the Albigenisan and Catharist heretics (DS *802). In 1863, Pope Pius IX confirmed the teaching, while noting that "invincible ignorance" can prevent the failure to enter the Church from being culpable (DS 2866-2867).

saved, who, through no fault of their own, are not aware of this necessity.[81]

8   Living a Good Life

8.1   *Keeping the Commandments*

There is more, however. Contrary to the opinion of some Protestant sects, the question of salvation does not come down to a simple act of faith in Christ, whether explicit or implicit, nor does simple membership in the Church suffice. One must also *follow* Christ, imitating His good life and obeying His "new commandment" of love.[82] The grace received at baptism enables the Christian to "walk in newness of life",[83] living with a dignity, purity and charity worthy of citizens of heaven. He is strengthened by the other sacraments, especially Confirmation and the Most Holy Eucharist, which is so essential that it, too, is

---

[81] The Catechism, with reference to the necessity of baptism for salvation, notes that anyone who would have been baptized had they known of the necessity, can be considered to have an implicit desire for baptism (CCC 1260). Pius IX reaffirmed long ago, that no one perishes but through their own fault.

[82] "By this all men will know that you are my disciples, if you have love for one another". Jn. 13:35.

[83] Rom. 6:4.

considered necessary for salvation: "Unless you eat my flesh and drink my blood you have no life in you."[84]

These sacraments, and other helps of which we will soon speak, are intended to bolster the sanctifying grace received at baptism, which included supernatural virtues and "gifts of the Holy Spirit".[85] All of these heavenly helps are designed to make us holy: "this is the will of God – your sanctification".[86] As a first step, they enable the recipient to keep the natural law, that is, to live a life worthy and becoming for our human nature. Due to the Fall, and the resulting tendency to sin with which we are conceived, this is not possible for long without the help of grace. Thus, it appears that even if a person does not

---

[84] John 6:53. Catholics believe that the bread and wine consecrated by the priest at Holy Mass become the Body, Blood, Soul and Divinity of Jesus Christ.

[85] Since our end (beatitude, union with God) exceeds our natural powers, our faculties (mind and will) need to be supernaturally assisted so as to tend to make correct choices. In order to act in a way that is even more efficacious for attaining our goal, we need to be moved by the Holy Spirit himself, and so are also endowed with "gifts of the Holy Spirit". These, too, are necessary for salvation, that is, again, for attaining a goal that is completely beyond our natural abilities.

[86] 1 Thess. 4:3.

reject Christ through his own fault, and even if he be justified in some unknown way, he will lack the many and great helps to salvation accessible through the Church. For this reason, St. Peter laments: "For the time has come for judgment to begin with the household of God; and if it begins with us, what will be the end of those who do not obey the gospel of God?"[87]

8.2   Mortal Sin

For indeed, notwithstanding their access to the sacraments, many Christians still struggle to observe the natural law precepts, which are represented by the Ten Commandments. Breaking such commandments means committing serious sin, which is called "mortal sin" precisely because the divine life received at baptism dies, and the accompanying supernatural gifts are lost. Consider the following explanation of the Council of Trent:

> ...the divine law ... excludes from the kingdom of God not only the unbelievers, but also the faithful who are *immoral, idolaters, adulterers, sexual perverts, thieves, greedy,*

---

[87] 1 Pet. 4:17. In support of this concern, St. Peter then quotes Proverbs 11:31: "If the righteous man is scarcely saved, where will the impious and sinner appear?"

> *drunkards, revilers, robbers* (cf. 1 Cor 6:9 ff.),
> and all others who commit deadly sins, from
> which with the assistance of divine grace
> they can refrain and for which they are sepa-
> rated from the grace of God.[88]

It is important to note that these laws are not arbitrary: sinful actions are not wrong because God prohibits them, but God prohibits them because they are wrong. Violations of the commandments are violations of basic, reasonable human behavior. God only prohibits us from doing what will harm us.[89] This truth, however, is hard to see, for, due to the Fall, many of the actions contrary to our rational nature are difficult for people to recognize as wrong. Hence, many will ardently defend actions that are blatantly contrary to the natural law such as abortion or same-sex behavior. We need God's help, which includes the guidance of the Magisterium of the Catholic Church,[90] to discover what

---

[88] DZ 1544.

[89] "Non enim Deus a nobis offenditur nisi ex eo quod contra nostrum bonum agimus ut dictum est." "God is offended by us only through what we do against our own good, as has been said" (Thomas Aquinas, SCG III, c. 122).

[90] "... as she contemplates the mystery of the Incarnate Word, the Church also comes to understand the 'mystery of man'; by proclaiming the Gospel of salvation, she reveals to man his dignity and invites him to discover fully the truth of

we should do, and also His help, especially through the sacraments, to do it.

Still, one cannot claim to be ignorant of these basic requirements for a human life pleasing to the Creator, since "what the law requires is written on [the Gentiles'] hearts".[91] In reference to this observation of St. Paul, then Cardinal Joseph Ratzinger noted soberly: "the whole theory of salvation through ignorance breaks apart with this verse."[92] For believers and unbelievers, a mortal sin does not require a conscious rejection of God, but simply a deliberate choice of something evil.[93]

---

his own being" (Instruction *Donum Vitae*, n. 1, Congregation for the Doctrine of the Faith, February 22, 1987).

[91] Rom. 2:15

[92] Ratzinger, "Conscience and Truth", presented at 10th Workshop for Bishops February 1991 Dallas, Texas (cf. http://www.ewtn.com/library/CURIA/RATZCONS.HTM).

[93] "[the act by which man freely and consciously rejects God] can occur in a direct and formal way, in the sins of idolatry, apostasy and atheism; or in an equivalent way, as in every act of disobedience to God's commandments in a grave matter" (*Reconciliatio et paenitentia*, n. 17).

8.3 *Growth in grace*

Consequently, in order to avoid sliding into sin and losing our share in divine life, we should seek to consolidate and increase it. St. Peter taught his early disciples that we can be confident of a happy eternity if we do: "Therefore, brethren, be the more zealous to confirm your call and election, for if you do this you will never fall; so there will be richly provided for you an entrance into the eternal kingdom of our Lord and Savior Jesus Christ."[94]

There are three ways by which to grow in grace. The first is the Sacraments. We mentioned the three "sacraments of initiation": Baptism, Confirmation and Most Holy Eucharist (or Holy Communion). In addition, there are two "sacraments of healing": Confession and Anointing of the Sick. These sacraments restore grace to the sinner and strengthen him against temptation. Finally, there are two sacraments which fortify a person for special roles in the Christian community: Priestly Orders and Marriage. The two sacraments which can be received frequently throughout life are Confession and Holy Communion.

---

[94] 2 Peter 1:10-11.

When they are received devoutly, they are mighty and continual sources of grace.

The second way of growing in grace is by "meritorious good works". In other words, any action which is performed for love of God by a person in a state of grace will merit an increase in grace. After all, the goal of the Christian life is not just to avoid offending God but to grow holy. Heaven is for saints. As St. Benedict's Rule tells us: "If we wish to attain a place in his kingdom, we shall not reach it unless we hasten there by our good works" (cf. Prologue).

Finally, the third way is prayer: by regular loving converse with God, a person will grow holy, even without realizing it. Included in prayer are many traditional Catholic practices and devotions, for instance, house blessings, using holy water, gaining indulgences, reciting the Divine Mercy Chaplet. Such things are optional helps offered to the faithful, but they can be very powerful in the struggle to remain and to grow in God's grace. A completely unparalleled place must be reserved for devotion to the Mother of God, the Blessed Virgin Mary. "Blessed, indeed, are those Christians who bind themselves faithfully and completely to her as to a secure anchor!... By an abundant outpouring of grace she keeps them from relaxing their effort in the practice of virtue or falling by the wayside through loss of divine grace."[95]

9   Final Perseverance

9.1   The Moment of Death

As the last moments of the life of the Good Thief demonstrate,[96] all that really matters is to finish well. One can "steal heaven" with an eleventh hour conversion, as Jesus teaches in the parable of the workers in the vineyard.[97] Many people, who have prayed the "Hail Mary" at some time – which concludes "Pray for us sinners now and at the hour of our death" – will surely experience God's great mercy towards sinners in their final hour. Nonetheless, it would be foolish to approach this decisive moment in your immortal existence ill prepared. Moreover, we can expect a particular battle with the Evil One, the enemy of

---

[95] St. Louis Marie de Montfort, *True Devotion to Mary*, n. 175 (Bay Shore, NY: Montfort Publications, 2006) p. 88-89.

[96] Luke 23:39-43.

[97] Matt. 20:1-16. A modern translation will speak of the last group of workers beginning at five o'clock instead of the literal "eleventh hour".

our souls, at this last moment. Therefore, we need to pray especially for the grace of "final perseverance", which is the assistance given by God so that a person effectively dies in the state of grace.[98] Then, even if we need to be purified of the remnants of sin and other imperfections in purgatory, our salvation and eternal happiness will be guaranteed.

9.2 Knowledge of Our Standing

The Church has definitively taught[99] that, barring a special revelation, no one can know for sure that he will die in a state of grace. Trent's teaching is a faithful echo of St. Thomas Aquinas's answer to the question "whether man can know he has grace" (I-II, q. 112, a. 5). In the body of that article, Aquinas specifies that one cannot know this "of himself ... and with certainty", but one

---

[98] Certain devotions to the Blessed Virgin, such as the wearing of the Brown Scapular or the making of the Five First Saturdays, not to mention Devotion to the Sacred Heart of Jesus, carry with them the promise of the grace of final perseverance. Since it is God's desire that we arrive safely and peacefully at the harbor, it is not surprising that He should offer even extraordinary helps to do so. This also helps one appreciate Indulgences, which are extraordinary helps to bypass the need for purgatory.

[99] Council of Trent, Session VI, can. 16 (DS 1566).

can know it by revelation or "conjecturally by signs".

Thus, we are not left in a state of pure ignorance regarding our standing before God — far from it. There are numerous signs that a person is still enjoying a real participation in the divine life: a well-formed conscience with no awareness of sin, virtues of humility, love of enemies, mercy to the suffering, a love of prayer, scripture, and devotion to the Blessed Virgin. Such evidence can give one confidence both about oneself and about others in whom such signs are observed. It is not arbitrary that all the world considered Mother Theresa a living saint. On the other hand, indifference to prayer and religious practice, breaking of commandments, disregard for the Blessed Virgin and other such signs give reason to fear an unhappy outcome. We cannot be absolutely sure in either case and so, in the former situation, the person should not cease to work out his salvation in fear and trembling,[100] while those in the latter situation should never despair nor be despaired of. It is important to remember that in the Lord's most famous parable about the

_____

[100] Phil. 2:12.

Last Judgment[101] both parties – those judged favorably and those condemned – were surprised by the verdict.

Nonetheless, a sober and realistic assessment can be made (which is distinct from the sins of judging and presumption), as indicated by an ancient Christian document, addressed to the Emperor Hadrian:

> And if any righteous man among [the Christians] passes from the world, they rejoice and offer thanks to God; and they escort his body as if he were setting out from one place to another near ... [but] if they see that any one of them dies in his ungodliness or in his sins, for him they grieve bitterly, and sorrow as for one who goes to meet his doom.[102]

Otherwise, we could neither look forward to judgment with hope and confidence, which is the goal of all the apostolic work of the Church, nor could we in charity warn and assist those living in sin.

---

[101] Matt. 25:31-46.
[102] Apology of Aristides (c. 125 a.d.)

9.3   How hard will this be?

Once a person recognizes Jesus Christ as Lord and the Catholic Church as His instrument in the work of salvation, the rest is relatively easy. The Church provides instruction in how to live virtuously, fonts of grace, models of sanctity and a community of like-minded pilgrims. With all this help, St John tells us, the commandments will not be "burdensome";[103] rather, we will grow in virtue, which makes it possible to choose the good "firmly, unhesitatingly and joyfully".[104] This tendency towards the good makes it difficult for a person to commit a mortal sin all of a sudden;[105] rather, such a grievous collapse would only come after a gradual decline through continued, deliberate venial sin and the abandonment of pious practices.

Nonetheless, experience proves that it is not so easy to persuade people of the necessity of faith in Christ and His Church, nor to keep them faithful to a commitment to them once made. As mentioned earlier, despite the fact that God

---

[103] 1 John 5:3.

[104] *firmiter, expedite, delectabiliter* (cf. St. Thomas *De virtutibus* 1, 1 s13; I-II q. 78, a. 3).

[105] *De virtutibus*, q.2, a.6, ad 1.

wishes all men to come to salvation, all men must choose the good path freely, contending with the three-fold enemy of their souls: the Devil,[106] the World[107] and their own fallen nature.

When the Lord was asked directly whether many would be saved, He replied: "Strive to enter by the narrow door; for many, I tell you, will seek to enter and will not be able."[108] This teaching was made still more explicit in the Gospel of Matthew: "Enter by the narrow gate; for the gate is wide and the way is easy, that leads to destruction, and those who enter by it are many. For the gate is narrow and the way is hard, that leads to life, and those who find it are few."[109]

St. Thomas Aquinas observes that speculating on this matter is imprudent: "Concerning the number of all the predestined ... it is however

---

[106] Certain angels, having rebelled against God, have turned definitively against all that is good, conceiving a great hatred for God and for persons seeking to love him.

[107] While the world is good insofar as it was created by God, the same term is used to refer to created things insofar as they distract and impede a person from seeking God. The 'world' would refer to all that is passing, superficial and enticing, and, in this sense, the Devil is called by Our Lord, "the Prince of this World" (Jn. 14:30).

[108] Luke 13:24

[109] Matt. 7:13-14.

better to say that 'to God alone is known the number for whom is reserved eternal happiness'".[110] Like the time the world will end, the answer is a secret known only to God. Nonetheless, just as we are not left entirely in the dark about the chances of any given individual, so also in general some prudential conjectures are possible. Not only the Lord's own words but a serious look at the attitudes and behaviors of most persons provide cause for the gravest concern. Does not Scripture refer to those who will be saved as the "elect"?[111] "Many are called, but few are chosen".[112] Once again, this does not

[110] *ST* I, q.23, a.7. Here St. Thomas quotes from the liturgy. For a correct understanding of the term 'predestined', see section 6.2.

[111] Mk 13:27, Lk 18:7, and elsewhere.

[112] Mt 22:14. For full disclosure, it must be admitted that in a recent encyclical (*Spe Salvi*, 2007), Pope Benedict XVI appears to make the unprecedented assertion that "the great majority of people – we may suppose" would be saved (cf. n. 46). This is accompanied by such a dramatic description of the sort of persons who would go to hell – "people who have totally destroyed their desire for truth and readiness to love, people for whom everything has become a lie, people who have lived for hatred and have suppressed all love within themselves" – that it could scarcely apply to anyone, although he alludes to "certain figures of our own history" as examples (cf. n. 45). These two numbers of the encyclical seem to be an attempt to

mean that God makes it very hard to enter into eternal life: we have seen, on the contrary, that every possible ordinary help and many extraordinary ones are provided. There remains, however, a mysterious resistance on the part of men: "[The Word] came to his own home, and his own people received him not".[113] Grace can be rejected. Love can be unrequited. The one who chooses badly can become definitively set upon his tragic turn inward.

10 Conclusion

Allow me, dear Reader, to congratulate you for having reached this point. You have accepted the invitation to consider the three most important questions in life. I dare to think that our reminder in the first chapter of the full scope of reason has permitted you to recognize yourself as part of a

---

repackage the Church's teaching on the Last Things for an audience that has ceased to believe in them. One must endeavor to read them in continuity with the Tradition, to which Pope Benedict directs us in a footnote: "To die in mortal sin without repenting and accepting God's merciful love means remaining separated from him forever by our own free choice." (CCC 1033). Regarding mortal sin, recall footnote 93.

[113] Jn. 1:11.

spiritual world, which lies beyond the ken of empirical science. Then, in the second chapter, you will have recognized that the possible destinies of our immortal soul could only be revealed by the One who made souls in His own image and came to lead them to a share in His life. Finally, in chapter three, you will have seen the wisdom of Christ's plan of founding on earth an institution – both human and divine – which could accompany those who would believe in Him to a safe harbor.

Is it not clear, then, that nothing remains but to surrender ourselves with perfect obedience to the Father, through Christ, in the holy Catholic Church? And then, after spending our lives in helping others to make the same discovery, we can lay down to the sleep of death with all the serenity of a child on his mother's breast,[114] dreaming of the morrow, that Day which breaks never to grow dim.

---

[114] Ps. 131:2.

Nemo potest idoneus fieri futurae vitae, qui non se ad illam modo exercuit.*

— St. Augustine

About the Author

Msgr. Andrew McLean Cummings, a priest of the Archdiocese of Baltimore, is currently serving at Mount Saint Mary's Seminary in Emmitsburg, Maryland.
He looks forward to sharing in the joys of heaven along with his twenty nieces and nephews.

————

*No one can be ready for the next life, unless he trains himself for it now.

CPSIA information can be obtained
at www.ICGtesting.com
Printed in the USA
LVHW081448030820
662249LV00017B/1935